ESCAPE ROOM PUZZLES
TOMB OF THE PHARAOHS

KINGFISHER
LONDON & NEW YORK

Copyright © Macmillan Publishers
International Ltd 2022
First published in 2022 by Kingfisher,
120 Broadway, New York, NY 10271
Kingfisher is an imprint of Macmillan
Children's Books, London
All rights reserved.

Distributed in the U.S. and Canada
by Macmillan, 120 Broadway,
New York, NY 10271

EU representative: Macmillan Publishers Ireland
Ltd, 1st Floor, The Liffey Trust Centre, 117-126
Sheriff Street Upper, Dublin 1, D01 YC43

Library of Congress
Cataloging-in-Publication
data has been applied for.

Written, designed, and illustrated
by Dynamo Limited

ISBN: 978-0-7534-7837-0

Kingfisher books are available for
special promotions and premiums.
For details contact: Special Markets
Department, Macmillan, 120 Broadway,
New York, NY 10271.

For more information, please visit
www.kingfisherbooks.com

Printed in China
9 8 7 6 5 4 3 2
2TR/0622/RV/WKT/120WF

MIX
Paper from
responsible sources
FSC® C116313

ESCAPE ROOM PUZZLES
TOMB OF THE PHARAOHS

KINGFISHER

LONDON & NEW YORK

CONTENTS

MEET THE TEAM!

Hey! I'm Kiran.

Ethan here!

NAME: Kiran

STRENGTHS: Leader and organizer

FUN FACT: Loves extreme sports—especially rock climbing

NAME: Ethan

STRENGTHS: Math and science genius

FUN FACT: Amazing memory for facts and always wins any quiz

Hello! Zane's the name.

Hi!

NAME: Zane

STRENGTHS: Creative and thinks outside the box

FUN FACT: Loves art and takes his trusty sketchbook wherever he goes

NAME: Cassia

STRENGTHS: Technology pro

FUN FACT: Queen of gadgets and invents her own apps

WELCOME!

Cassia, Zane, Ethan, and Kiran are always finding themselves on out-of-this-world adventures. But where are they this time?

Their journey starts in Egypt—they're on a school trip visiting the Tomb of the Pharaohs. Now, a school trip to Egypt sounds epic in itself, but you can be sure that things will take an unexpected turn when these four are around!

Ethan's mother, Jess, is an archaeologist who worked on a site in Egypt when she was young. Jess has told Ethan lots of stories about the tomb, including her biggest regret: how she'd never managed to restore an ancient artifact. The story goes that someone removed the precious stones from the artifact in order to steal them, but failed miserably, so today the stones are scattered within the tomb walls. The artifact must be restored by returning the missing stones or else the entire tomb will soon collapse and be swallowed up by sand. Years later, the task remains uncompleted and time is running out ... fast!

YOUR MISSION:
Once inside the tomb, you must sneak away from your classmates, find the precious stones, and return them to the artifact—all without your teacher noticing you've gone. The tomb is riddled with hidden passages, traps, and mazes—not to mention mummies! You must work together to save the tomb, if you dare ...

WHAT YOU KNOW:

☥ There is an underground passage within the tomb that you must find to complete the mission.

☥ You're armed with an ancient crumpled map of the tomb that Ethan found in his mother's study.

☥ In the corner of the map is a symbol that Ethan's mother sketched during her time there.

Important!
Look out for precious stones as you move through the tomb. You need to find 10 altogether if you're going to complete the mission.

ROOM ONE:
TOMB ENTRANCE

Welcome to the Tomb of the Pharaohs. It's the day you've all been waiting for—you're finally here! Your tour guide is waiting at the entrance to the tomb. The whole class excitedly follows the teacher and tour guide through the grand entrance. As you step inside, Cassia and Kiran immediately start looking for clues, while Zane busily tries to sketch everything he sees.

You find yourself at the top of an enormous limestone ramp that looks surprisingly sturdy for how long ago it was built. The tour guide leads everybody down, deeper into the tomb. It's so much cooler down here than it was in the entrance passageway. As soon as the tour guide starts to list the day's activities, Cassia, Ethan, Kiran, and Zane begin their mission. Tucked away under the large staircase is a curtain of patterned fabric. Ethan pulls it to one side to discover what looks like a secret exit. It's covered in cobwebs! He gives the door a push, but nothing happens. Is their mission over before it's even begun?

NUMBER NIGHTMARE

While the rest of the class listens to the tour guide, you must use this time to crack the first puzzle and unlock the door. Luckily, Ethan has spotted an ancient-looking keypad beside the door. Can you fill in the missing numbers to solve the sums on page 11?

Each line has to add up to a certain amount. Let's fill in the blanks.

Write the missing numbers in the spaces so that each set adds up to the correct amount.

I'll try a few combinations in my sketchbook.

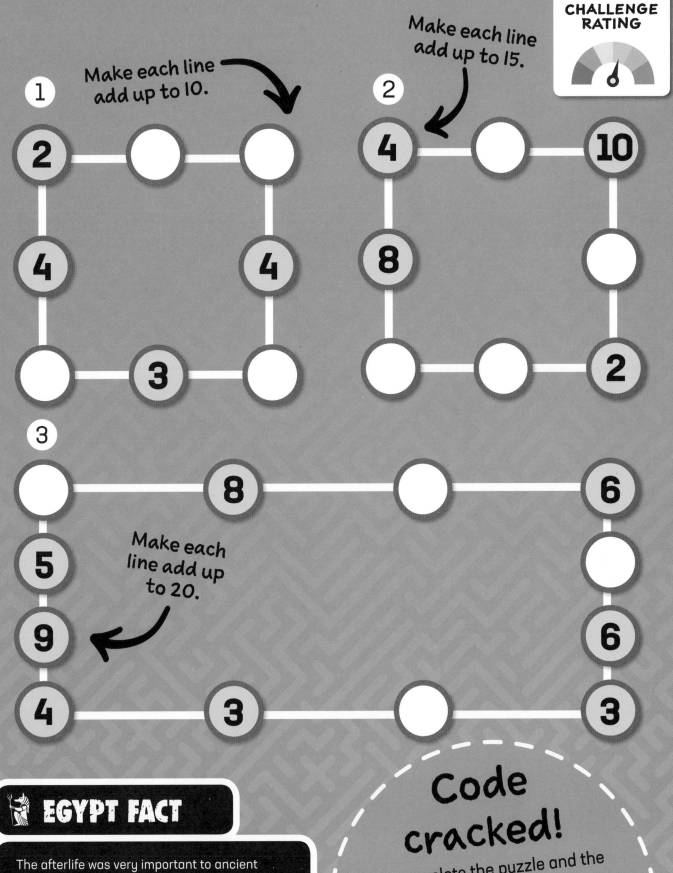

1 Make each line add up to 10.

2 — — —
4 — 4
— 3 —

2 Make each line add up to 15.

4 — 10
8 —
— — 2

3 Make each line add up to 20.

— 8 — 6
5 — 6
9 — 6
4 — 3 — 3

EGYPT FACT

The afterlife was very important to ancient Egyptians. They believed that mummification would allow the souls of the dead to live on forever after they died.

Code cracked!

You complete the puzzle and the door clicks open. What awaits you on the other side?

BOULDER ROLL

The door opens into a long, dark corridor. Kiran is leading the way up ahead when she reaches a boulder blocking the path. For this challenge, you must roll the boulder through the maze so that you can smash through the crumbling stone wall at the finish line.

Use a pencil to work out the best route to get the boulder from the top to the finish. Dodge the piles of boulders to avoid the boulder getting stuck.

START

IT'S ALIVE!

You follow the beeping from Cassia's tablet until it brings you to a huge tapestry hanging on a wall. Zane leans in to take a closer look and notices something strange ... Uh oh, it's crawling with live scarab beetles!

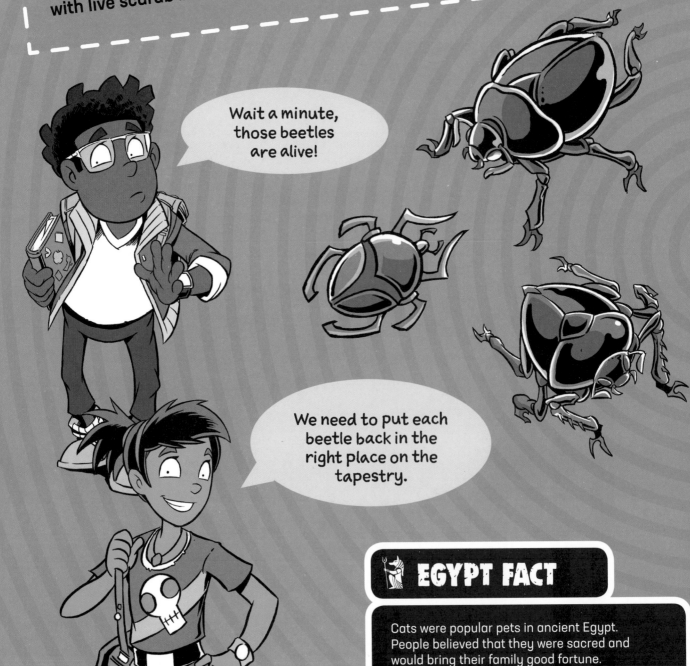

Wait a minute, those beetles are alive!

We need to put each beetle back in the right place on the tapestry.

EGYPT FACT

Cats were popular pets in ancient Egypt. People believed that they were sacred and would bring their family good fortune.

Draw lines to show where each beetle fits.

 ①  ②  ③ ④ ⑤

Phew!

You didn't let this one beat you. As the final beetle is put in place, the tapestry moves to reveal the antechamber entrance. There's no time to lose, so you all follow Kiran inside.

ROOM TWO:
ENTER THE ANTECHAMBER

With those creepy crawlies safely back in their place on the tapestry, it's time to enter the antechamber. This part of the tomb seems like the perfect place for the missing artifact to be hiding. It's the largest room in the tomb and packed full of ancient Egyptian treasures. But are any of them the one you're looking for to complete the mission? There are extravagant thrones, animal-shaped couches, and huge chests everywhere you look—and you need to investigate all of them!

Remember to keep your focus—there's no time for distractions, and the longer your mission takes, the more danger there is of someone noticing that you're missing!

SAFE SUMS

After rummaging around for clues, Ethan finds a safe in the corner of the room, alongside a rolled-up scroll on the floor. To open the safe, you must complete this number challenge using the clues on the scroll to help you. Before you can solve the sums, you must work out the value of each shape.

Ha! Ha! Ha!

Why did the Egyptians build pyramids?

Because their igloos melted.

I think the answer has something to do with the number of sides on the shapes.

READY, SET, SEARCH!

You have the key, but no clue what to do next. Cassia decides to turn on the tracking device on her tablet. As she does that, the tablet brings up a series of pictures. It's asking the team to find each item in the room and scan it into the device.

Tick off each of these items when you find it hidden in the picture.

Lucky find!

Zane is so busy sketching that
he almost misses the next stone.
Can you find it? You'll need it.

TRICKY TRIO

You scan the last item into Cassia's tablet and another screen pops up. This time, it shows three elaborate thrones—but can you find the odd one out?

Isn't this the same symbol that Ethan's mom sketched onto the corner of that map?

🔱 EGYPT FACT

The ancient Egyptians were skilled inventors. They invented pens, locks for doors, a kind of paper called papyrus, and even toothpaste.

You're right! That must be the throne we should choose!

Nailed it!

At last, Cassia selects the odd throne out—challenge successfully completed! Suddenly, there's a loud rumble and one of the ancient tomb walls slides to the side. What's behind it?

PYRAMID DROP

The wall slides to reveal what looks like a giant board game laid out on the floor. At the end of the game is the throne from the picture. You need to figure out which beetle to start from to take you to it. Play by the rules, or you might just be dropped into the depths of the tomb!

Rules

☥ You can't move to a pyramid of the same color.

☥ You must follow the lines and cannot move diagonally—break this rule and the pyramid you're on will collapse and you will fall into the depths of the tomb.

Let's think about this logically. Don't rush!

You can only move along these lines.

Risky!

That was close—but you made it! As you all scramble over to the throne, you notice a hidden doorway behind it—but where does it lead?

ROOM THREE:
THE ANNEX

Congratulations! You successfully avoided the dreaded pyramid drop. If you can survive that, who knows what you're capable of? But it's not over yet. You still need to locate those remaining precious stones. Without them, you'll have no chance of restoring the ancient artifact and saving the tomb from sinking away forever.

You're now in the annex. Unlike the enormous antechamber that you've just left behind, this room is seriously cramped! In fact, it's the smallest room in the entire tomb. But don't go thinking there won't be much here to keep you busy. The room may be teeny-tiny, but there's plenty to explore. Every space is filled with beautiful pottery, oils, and other trinkets.

Cassia, Ethan, Kiran, and Zane waste no time and set off to explore. Hurry up, you don't want to be left behind!

VOLUME UP

The first thing you discover in this room is a pair of scales. Each side is loaded with jugs containing mysterious liquids. Look carefully and you'll see that weights are written on the jugs, except for one! The scales must balance exactly, so you need to figure out how much liquid you should pour into the final jar to make them balance.

Work out your answer here!

There is another precious stone in this room somewhere. Can you find it? Hang onto it, you'll need it later.

What's this?

As the scales balance, you hear something click into place. While everyone's busy looking for the source of the noise, Zane notices something underneath a shelf. It's a small padlocked doorway.

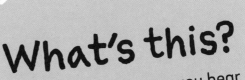

BOLT BREAKER

It looks like the door is double-locked! To open the padlock you must first crack the number code below. Look at the answers that have been filled in for you and use them to help you complete the last sum.

Somebody really doesn't want anyone getting in that room!

Math? This looks like my kind of challenge!

Work out your answer here!

Now what?

You crack the code and enter the numbers into the padlock—but nothing happens. Everyone feels like giving up, until Zane remembers the small key you found earlier. The key fits! With a smooth turn of the lock, the door swings open.

SAVE THE SCROLL

Once everyone is through the door, Zane spots an ancient-looking scroll. He carefully unrolls it to reveal hieroglyphs and other symbols. But the scroll is so old that parts of it fall away. Can you help put the missing pieces back together?

Hold onto that scroll, Zane. I think we'll need it!

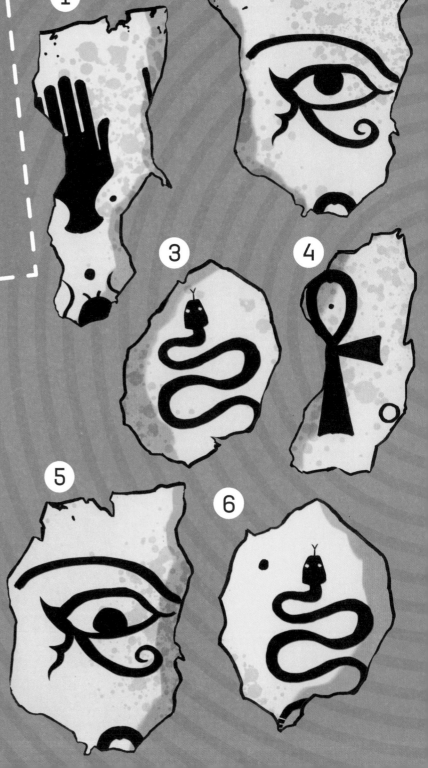

Write the correct numbers in the spaces to show where each piece fits.

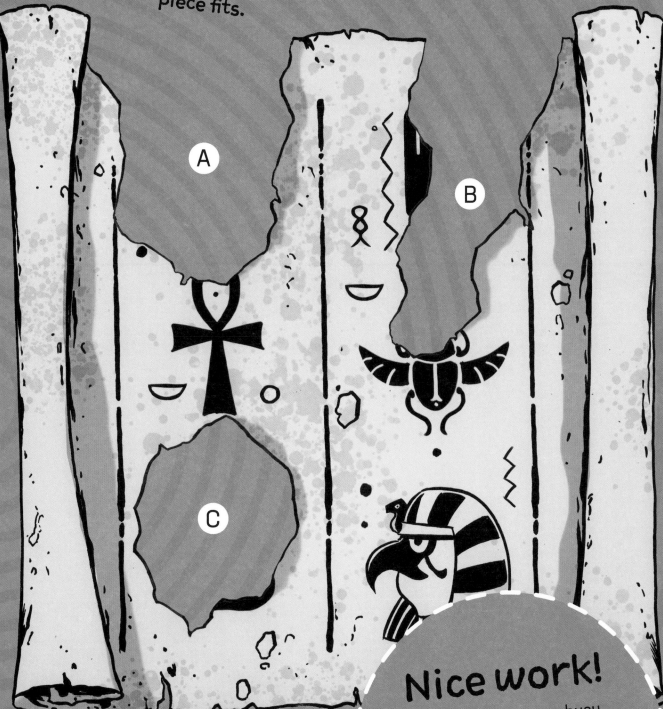

A

B

C

Nice work!

While the others are busy completing the last parts of the scroll, Cassia finds the entrance to some sort of maze. It's time to explore ...

MUMMY MAZE

Are you ready to brave the ancient maze? Be sure to dodge the mummies as you make your way through each corridor. And don't miss the hieroglyphs along the way—you must pass all four symbols to move forward in your mission.

Hieroglyphs

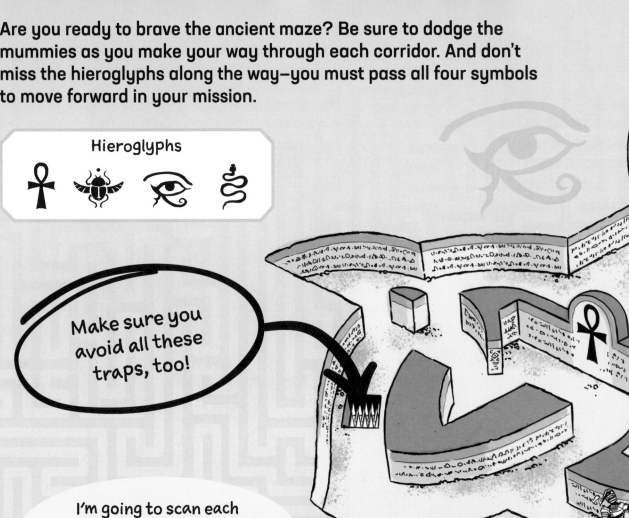

Make sure you avoid all these traps, too!

I'm going to scan each hieroglyph into my app in the order that we pass them.

START

FINISH

CHALLENGE
RATING

DON'T pass through
the same part of the
maze twice!

Hooray!
Cassia scans the final
hieroglyph into her app as
you all breeze through the
exit. Suddenly, her tablet
lights up ...

SHIFTING SYMBOLS

As you enter the next room, Cassia's tablet lights up with a grid. It looks like your task is to fill in the blank spaces using the four hieroglyphs you collected in the maze.

This reminds me of a sudoku puzzle. Maybe that will help?

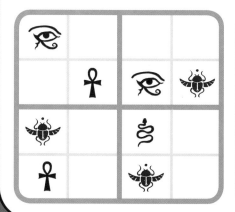

Draw the hieroglyphs or fill in their corresponding numbers to complete the grid.

Remember that each symbol can only appear once in each column, row, and square.

Awesome!

With all of the symbols in the correct place, a bolt shifts and a door slowly creaks open. What will the next room have in store?

 EGYPT FACT

Ancient Egyptians wrote using a system of pictures and symbols called hieroglyphics. The word hieroglyphics means "holy writings" and the individual symbols are called hieroglyphs.

ROOM FOUR:
THE BURIAL CHAMBER

Excellent work, team! You've dodged a maze full of terrifying mummies, solved a sudoku grid, and cracked codes—and it's all paid off because now you've made it through another room. But things are taking longer than expected. You must speed up if you don't want your class teacher to miss you. Plus, you still need to restore the missing artifact before the whole tomb sinks!

You now find yourself in the burial chamber. This grand room is filled with bright colors and huge murals cover the walls. What's more, there are extravagant shrines everywhere! Here you'll find coffins made from solid gold, not to mention the famous death masks. It's less cluttered than the last room—let's just hope that makes it easier to track down the remaining precious stones.

Are you ready for your next challenge?

SWITCH OFF

You all rush into the burial chamber but quickly stop in your tracks. Ahead of you is a wall of lasers. This is getting dangerous! Suddenly, Cassia's tablet vibrates, and a keypad appears on the screen. There's only one way to get out of this precarious situation—you must deactivate the lasers by typing in the correct code.

Start on the * key and follow the instructions carefully to figure out which keys to press:

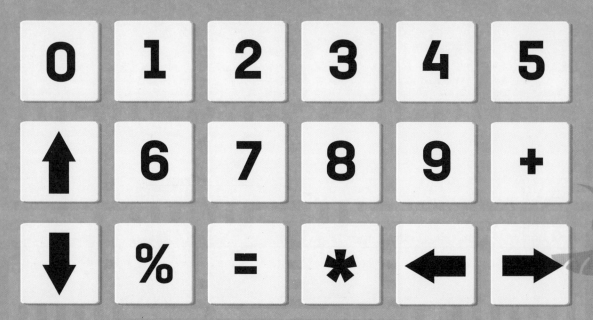

0	1	2	3	4	5
↑	6	7	8	9	+
↓	%	=	*	←	→

Instructions:
- ☥ Move up one key
- ☥ Move right two keys
- ☥ Move up one key
- ☥ Move left 4 keys
- ☥ Move down 1 key
- ☥ Move left 1 key

CHALLENGE RATING

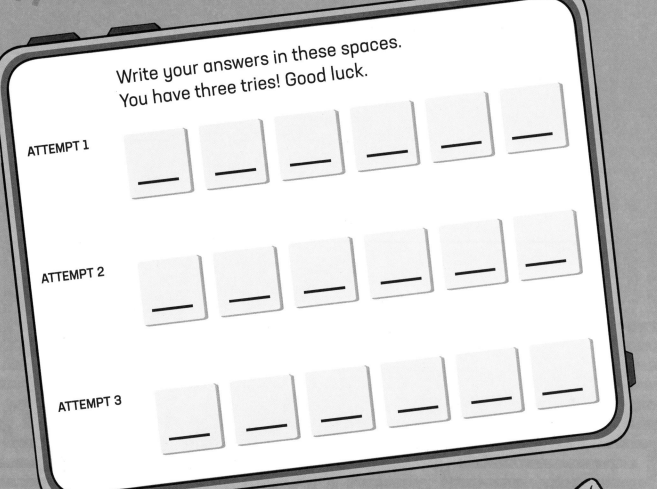

Write your answers in these spaces.
You have three tries! Good luck.

ATTEMPT 1

ATTEMPT 2

ATTEMPT 3

This app I've created is really coming in handy.

Deactivated!

That was incredible.
The lasers are safely
deactivated and you're
able to move forward
in your mission.

SPOT THE DIFFERENCE

Now those pesky lasers have been dealt with, it's time to step further into the burial chamber. Zane gets excited when he catches sight of a real-life death mask and shrine. He immediately recognizes it from a drawing he did in class when they were preparing for the trip. But something isn't quite right. Some things on the real mask and shrine are different. Can you spot them?

Look, there's another stone!

Circle each difference as you go! There are 10 to find altogether.

Eagle eye!

As the team study the death mask, it becomes clear that this is where the stones need to be returned! This is the artifact that you've been trying to restore.

DON'T BE ALARMED!

As Kiran walks toward the death mask, a piercing ringing sound stops her in her tracks. You all take a look around and see that there are four alarms blaring out, making it hard for you to think or even move! Each alarm must be switched off in the right order before the stones can be replaced on the mask.

Read the instructions to color in the squares in each grid and reveal a number.

Red alarm

1	2	3	4	5	6	7	8	9	10
11	12	13	14	15	16	17	18	19	20
21	22	23	24	25	26	27	28	29	30
31	32	33	34	35	36	37	38	39	40
41	42	43	44	45	46	47	48	49	50
51	52	53	54	55	56	57	58	59	60
61	62	63	64	65	66	67	68	69	70
71	72	73	74	75	76	77	78	79	80
81	82	83	84	85	86	87	88	89	90
91	92	93	94	95	96	97	98	99	100

Color in these numbers **red**:

3, 4, 5, 6, 16, 26, 36, 44, 45, 46, 56, 66, 76, 86, 93, 94, 95, 96

Blue alarm

Color in these numbers **blue**:

4, 5, 6, 13, 17, 23, 27, 33, 37, 44, 46, 55, 64, 66, 73, 77, 83, 87, 94, 95, 96

1	2	3	4	5	6	7	8	9	10
11	12	13	14	15	16	17	18	19	20
21	22	23	24	25	26	27	28	29	30
31	32	33	34	35	36	37	38	39	40
41	42	43	44	45	46	47	48	49	50
51	52	53	54	55	56	57	58	59	60
61	62	63	64	65	66	67	68	69	70
71	72	73	74	75	76	77	78	79	80
81	82	83	84	85	86	87	88	89	90
91	92	93	94	95	96	97	98	99	100

Yellow alarm

1	2	3	4	5	6	7	8	9	10
11	12	13	14	15	16	17	18	19	20
21	22	23	24	25	26	27	28	29	30
31	32	33	34	35	36	37	38	39	40
41	42	43	44	45	46	47	48	49	50
51	52	53	54	55	56	57	58	59	60
61	62	63	64	65	66	67	68	69	70
71	72	73	74	75	76	77	78	79	80
81	82	83	84	85	86	87	88	89	90
91	92	93	94	95	96	97	98	99	100

Color in these numbers **yellow**:

5, 6, 14, 16, 23, 26, 33, 36, 43, 46, 54, 55, 56, 66, 76, 86, 96

Color in these numbers **green**:

4, 5, 6, 7, 17, 27, 37, 47, 57, 67, 77, 87, 97

Green alarm

1	2	3	4	5	6	7	8	9	10
11	12	13	14	15	16	17	18	19	20
21	22	23	24	25	26	27	28	29	30
31	32	33	34	35	36	37	38	39	40
41	42	43	44	45	46	47	48	49	50
51	52	53	54	55	56	57	58	59	60
61	62	63	64	65	66	67	68	69	70
71	72	73	74	75	76	77	78	79	80
81	82	83	84	85	86	87	88	89	90
91	92	93	94	95	96	97	98	99	100

We now have four numbers, but how does it help us?

My app says to turn off the alarms by putting the numbers in order from smallest to biggest.

Write the correct order of the alarms here.

___ ___ ___ ___

Hit the switch!

As you switch off the alarms, Zane hears a sound underfoot. He looks down to find a pouch with some more precious stones inside. Do these need to be put back in the death mask, too?

DEATH MASK

Now there's nothing to stop you restoring that artifact! All that's left to do is put the missing pieces back in their rightful places. Sounds simple, right? Well, you have 10 stones (plus the extras that Zane picked up), and your next challenge is to work out exactly where each one fits.

B C D E F

G H I J K L

M N O P Q R

CHALLENGE RATING

Once a stone is in place, it sets. We get no second chances.

Yeah, we only get one shot!

Can you identify the missing stones?

Aced it!

Phew, that was SO tricky, but you've actually done it. Mission complete! Now there's one thing left to do—you've got to get back to your classmates.

ROOM FIVE:
SECRET PASSAGE

You're so close to completing the mission—thanks to the team, the tomb is now safe from being swallowed up by the desert sand and lost forever. Ethan can't wait to surprise his mom with the good news, but before he can do that, you still have to find your way back out from the depths of the tomb!

Years ago, Ethan's mom told him stories about a secret underground passageway in the tomb. She said that the passageway was marked with a pyramid symbol, and all that you needed to do was follow it to find your way out safely.

Kiran immediately starts rushing around the room in search of a pyramid symbol and soon spots it high up on the tomb wall! Beneath the mysterious symbol are four doorways. Only one of them will lead you back to your classmates, who are now almost at the end of their guided tour. Time is running out!

UR DOORS, THREE TRAPS

There are four doors to choose from, but only one will reveal the secret passageway out of the tomb. The other routes are riddled with traps and lead to dead ends! Which door should you choose? As you stand in front of them, you notice that each one has a different symbol on it ...

Hey, one of them matches the symbol on the map!

Each symbol is a top-down view of a pyramid.

EGYPT FACT

Ancient Egyptians were big fans of board games. Their version of dice were called "knuckle bones" or "throw sticks."

Your challenge is to figure out which symbol matches the pyramid on the map.

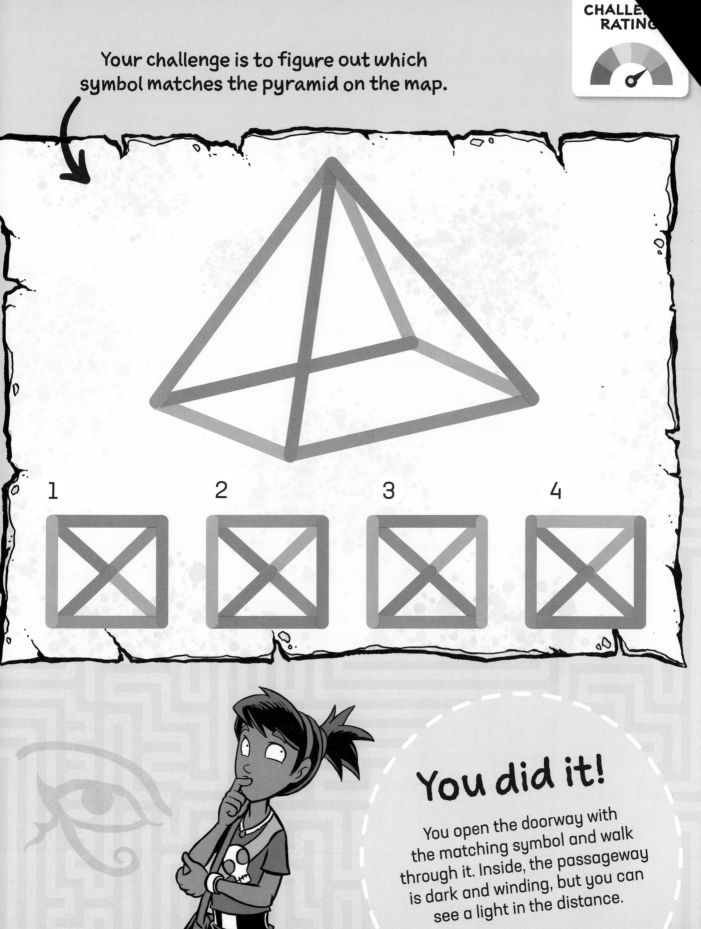

1   2   3   4

You did it!

You open the doorway with the matching symbol and walk through it. Inside, the passageway is dark and winding, but you can see a light in the distance.

SKETCH IT!

You all frantically scramble down the passageway toward the light and emerge in what appears to be the treasury. Zane grabs his sketchbook and excitedly starts doodling a set of canopic jars he has spotted. Grab a pencil and get drawing to make his sketch match the scene exactly!

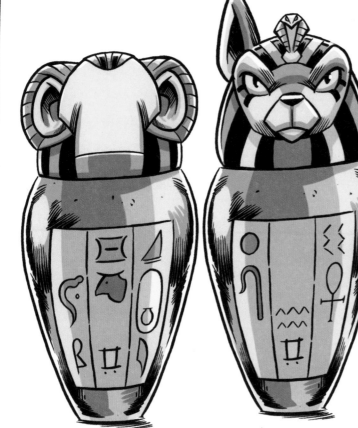

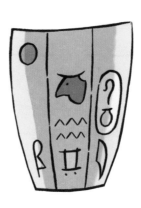

These are incredible. I have to sketch them!

My app might be able to translate those hieroglyphs!

Be quick!

As Zane draws, Cassia studies the hieroglyphs on one of the canopic jars and quickly scans them into her device ...

ANAGRAM ANTICS

As soon as Cassia has scanned the hieroglyphs, her app brings up a series of anagrams. Suddenly, you hear a mysterious ticking noise start up from somewhere in the room. It's a race against the clock to rearrange the words. Too slow and all the letters will disappear! Can you help the team solve this?

Hint
Each word has an ancient Egyptian theme!

We need to rearrange these letters into words before we can go any further.

1 oharahp

2 shpnix

3 rseature

4 rhinse

5 dyrapmi

6 dgdesos

1 _____

2 _____

3 _____

4 _____

5 _____

6 _____

Fill in your answers here!

Cracked it!

You solve the final anagram, and then a message appears on Cassia's tablet: "*Rearrange the tiles to discover who is hidden ...*"

EGYPT FACT

The ancient Egyptians worshipped over 2,000 gods and goddesses. Many of them were depicted as humans with animal heads.

MBLED DISGUISE

After searching high and low, Kiran eventually finds a portrait of a goddess made from tiles on a far wall—but some of the tiles are missing! You look around and see that a number of tiles have fallen to the floor. Can you figure out which ones fit the gaps?

Write the correct letters in the spaces to complete the portrait.

Good luck!

Alrighty, let's work out which tiles fit where.

 EGYPT FACT

Not all ancient Egyptians were mummified.
It was very expensive and took a long time,
so it was only for the richest people.

Awesome!

The goddess portrait was disguising the exit all along. As you slide the final tile into place, the portrait parts to reveal four more doors.

OCKED OUT

Each door has a number painted on it, along with a picture of some blocks. But how does that help you? On the correct door, the number at the top should match the number of blocks in the picture—that's the door you need!

Ha! Ha! Ha!

Did you hear about the stressed-out mummy? He was all wound up!

Beep, beep!

Cassia's app begins to make a beeping noise—it's the reminder she set, meaning your classmates are due to leave the tomb in five minutes! Go, go, go!

RAVELING

As you rush hastily through the correct door, you fall into a tangle of unraveling mummy bandages. Yikes! Your task is to find which one leads you out of this room and back to your classmates.

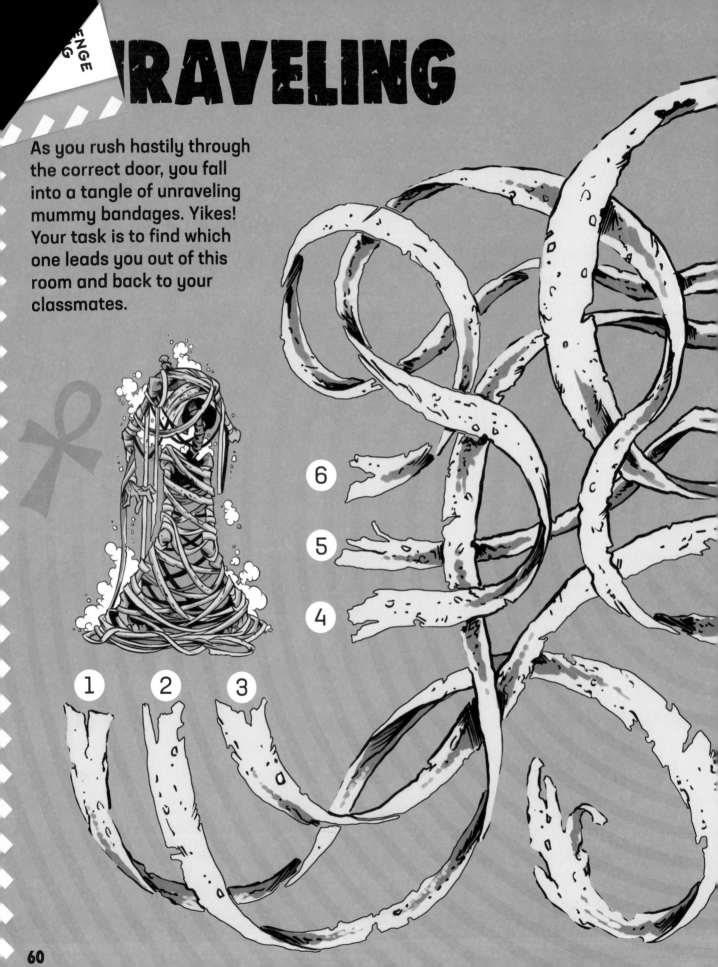

Look, everyone—
there's the exit!
We're so close.

Let's see where
each bandage
takes us!

Unbelievable!

Finally, you make it back to your class and try to act like you've been there the whole time! As you rejoin the group, the guide makes an announcement:
"While we were on our tour today, the clock was reset and this ancient tomb has been saved. It's no longer in danger of being lost forever in the desert sands. We don't know who managed to lift the curse ... but it's a miracle!"

SWERS

PAGES 10-11
1: TOP LINE: **5, 3**
   BOTTOM LINE: **4, 3**

2: TOP LINE: **1**
   RIGHT LINE: 3
   BOTTOM LINE: **3, 10**

3: TOP LINE: **2, 4**
   RIGHT LINE: **5**
   BOTTOM LINE: **10**

PAGES 12-13

PAGES 14-15

PAGES 18-19
1: **18**   2: **10**   3: **26**

PAGES 20-21

PAGES 22-23

PAGES 24-25

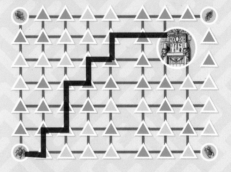

PAGES 28-29
The answer is 30

PAGES 30-31
The answer is 20

PAGES 32-33
A: **2**   B: **1**   C: **6**

PAGES 34-35

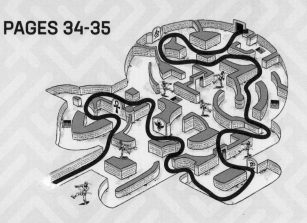

PAGES 36-37

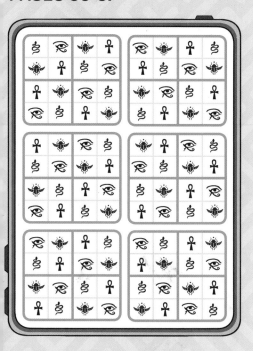

PAGES 40-41

8 + 516↑

PAGES 42-43

PAGES 44-45

The correct order for the alarms is: 3 7 8 9

PAGES 46-47

1: **Q**   2: **A**   3: **I**   4: **J**   5: **O**   6: **K**
7: **M**   8: **H**   9: **R**   10: **B**

PAGES 50-51

The answer is 3

PAGES 54-55

1: **pharaoh**
2: **sphinx**
3: **treasure**
4: **shrine**
5: **pyramid**
6: **goddess**

PAGES 56-57

A: **4**   B: **9**   C: **8**   D: **2**

PAGES 58-59

This is the correct door

PAGES 60-61

SEE YOU ON THE NEXT ADVENTURE!

Color in the team!